THE AI MARKETING PLAYBOOK

The AI Marketing Playbook

Dots McGuyen

Contents

1

Introduction to AI in Small Business

UNDERSTANDING AI AND ITS IMPACT ON SMALL BUSINESSES

Understanding AI and its impact on small businesses requires an exploration of how artificial intelligence technologies can transform various aspects of operations, marketing, and customer engagement. For small business owners and content creators, AI offers innovative solutions that can streamline processes, enhance productivity, and provide valuable insights. By leveraging AI-powered tools, these businesses can compete more effectively in a crowded marketplace, making it essential to grasp the capabilities and limitations of these technologies.

AI programs specifically designed for small businesses can automate repetitive tasks, allowing owners to focus on strategic initiatives. For instance, AI virtual assistants can manage scheduling, customer inquiries, and even social media interactions, freeing up time for more important tasks. Furthermore, AI-powered marketing tools can analyze customer behavior and preferences, enabling businesses to tailor their marketing strategies to meet specific needs. This level of personalization is key in building customer loyalty and driving sales.

In addition to marketing, smart inventory management systems powered by AI can optimize stock levels and supply chain processes. These systems use predictive analytics to forecast demand, reducing overstock and stockouts. This not only helps in maintaining a healthier cash flow but also enhances customer satisfaction by ensuring product availability. Small business owners can thus make data-driven decisions that lead to improved operational efficiency and profitability.

Financial planning and budgeting are other critical areas where AI can make a significant impact. AI-enhanced tools can analyze financial data, predict future trends, and help in creating accurate budgets. By automating these financial processes, small businesses can gain insights that were previously difficult to obtain, enabling more informed decision-making. This level of financial clarity can be a game-changer for small businesses that often operate with limited resources.

Lastly, AI-driven SEO optimization tools and personalized email marketing automation can greatly enhance online visibility and customer engagement. These technologies provide insights into search trends and customer behaviors, allowing businesses to craft content that resonates with their target audience. By utilizing AI for social media management and content curation, small business owners can maintain a consistent online presence while optimizing their marketing efforts. In summary, understanding AI and its multifaceted impact is crucial for small business owners and content creators looking to harness its potential for growth and success.

THE IMPORTANCE OF AI FOR SMALL BUSINESS GROWTH

The integration of artificial intelligence (AI) into small business operations marks a transformative era in how these enterprises can grow and thrive. Small businesses, often constrained by limited resources, can leverage AI to enhance efficiency, optimize marketing strategies, and improve customer engagement. By adopting AI technologies, small business owners can automate routine tasks, allowing them to focus on core activities that drive growth. This shift not only streamlines operations but also reduces overhead costs, creating a more sustainable business model.

AI-powered marketing tools offer small businesses a competitive advantage by enabling personalized marketing campaigns that resonate with target audiences. Utilizing data-driven insights, these tools can help business owners tailor their messaging, ensuring that it aligns with customer preferences and behaviors. This level of personalization fosters deeper connections with customers, leading to higher engagement rates and increased loyalty. As small business owners harness the power of AI in their marketing efforts, they can expect improved conversion rates and a better return on investment.

In the realm of content creation and curation, AI technologies can assist small business owners in generating high-quality content that attracts and retains customers. AI-based tools can analyze trending topics, identify gaps in content, and even generate written material that aligns with the brand's voice. This capability not only saves time but also ensures that businesses consistently provide valuable content to their audience. As content is a key driver of digital marketing success, leveraging AI in this area can significantly enhance a small business's online presence.

Smart inventory management systems powered by AI can revolutionize how small businesses handle their stock levels, reducing waste and optimizing supply chains. These systems use predictive analytics to forecast demand, ensuring that businesses maintain the right amount of inventory at all times. By avoiding overstocking and stockouts, small business owners can enhance customer satisfaction and improve cash flow. The application of AI in inventory management is particularly beneficial for small retailers and e-commerce businesses, where inventory turnover is crucial to profitability.

Finally, AI-driven financial planning and budgeting tools provide small business owners with the insights needed to make informed financial decisions. These tools can analyze historical data, predict future trends, and assist in creating robust financial strategies. Additionally, personalized email marketing automation powered by AI can help businesses maintain communication with customers, fostering relationships that drive repeat sales. By embracing AI across various aspects of their operations, small business owners can navigate challenges more effectively and unlock new avenues for growth.

2

AI Programs for Small Business and Creators

OVERVIEW OF AI PROGRAMS AVAILABLE

In the rapidly evolving landscape of digital marketing, small business owners and content creators are increasingly turning to artificial intelligence (AI) programs to enhance their operations and drive growth. The variety of AI tools available today can be overwhelming, but understanding the key programs tailored for small businesses can empower owners to make informed decisions. These programs encompass a wide range of functions, from content creation and curation to inventory management and financial planning, each designed to streamline processes and improve efficiency.

One of the most prominent categories of AI tools is AI-powered marketing solutions. These tools leverage machine learning algorithms to analyze consumer behavior and preferences, allowing businesses to craft personalized marketing campaigns. Small business owners can utilize these platforms to automate email marketing, ensuring targeted messaging reaches customers at the right time. Additionally, AI-driven social media management tools help businesses optimize their online presence by analyzing engagement metrics and suggesting content strategies to boost visibility and interaction.

Content creation and curation are other vital areas where AI programs shine. These tools assist in generating high-quality, relevant content tailored to target audiences, saving time and resources for small businesses and creators. By analyzing trends and popular topics, AI can suggest content ideas and even produce written material, freeing up creative professionals to focus on strategy and engagement. Moreover, AI-enhanced SEO optimization tools help businesses improve their online visibility by providing insights into keyword performance and search engine rankings, ensuring that content reaches its intended audience.

Inventory management and financial planning are essential for maintaining a healthy business operation. AI-powered inventory systems can predict stock needs based on historical data and trends, minimizing overstock and stockouts while optimizing cash flow. Similarly, AI-driven financial planning tools offer insights into budgeting and forecasting, enabling small business owners to make data-driven decisions that align with their growth objectives. These innovations help reduce the complexity of financial management, allowing owners to focus more on strategic initiatives.

Finally, the integration of predictive analytics into business strategy is transforming how small businesses approach growth. By analyzing historical data, predictive analytics tools can identify patterns and forecast future trends, equipping owners with the insights needed to make proactive decisions. This allows for more effective resource allocation and marketing strategies. Additionally, virtual assistants powered by AI can automate routine tasks, enhancing productivity by allowing small business owners to concentrate on core activities that drive growth. As technology continues to advance, these AI programs offer invaluable support for small businesses striving to thrive in a competitive environment.

SELECTING THE RIGHT AI PROGRAM FOR YOUR NEEDS

Selecting the right AI program for your needs begins with a clear understanding of your business objectives. Small business owners and content creators should identify the specific challenges they face and determine how AI can address these issues. For instance, if your primary concern is streamlining marketing efforts, you might explore AI-powered marketing tools that automate customer engagement and enhance targeting. Conversely, if content creation is your focus, programs that specialize in AI-based content creation and curation will be more relevant. By aligning your AI selection with your goals, you can ensure that the technology not only fits your operational needs but also contributes to your overall growth strategy.

Next, consider the scalability of the AI tools you are evaluating. Small businesses often operate with limited resources, so it is crucial to choose AI programs that can grow alongside your business. Look for solutions that offer flexible pricing models, allowing you to start with essential features and expand as your needs evolve. Tools that integrate well with your existing systems will also save time and reduce the complexity of implementation. This scalability will provide you with the confidence that your investment in AI technology will yield long-term benefits, adapting as your business landscape changes.

User-friendliness is another critical factor in selecting the right AI program. Many small business owners and content creators may not have extensive technical expertise, so it's essential to choose tools that are intuitive and easy to navigate. Programs that offer robust customer support and comprehensive training resources can significantly reduce the learning curve associated with new technology. Additionally, consider platforms that feature customizable dashboards and reporting capabilities, which allow you to easily access and analyze data relevant to your marketing and operational efforts.

Integration capabilities should also play a significant role in your decision-making process. The ideal AI program will seamlessly connect with your existing software, whether it's your customer relationship management system, accounting software, or content management platform. This integration ensures that you can leverage data across different tools, leading to more informed decision-making and enhanced efficiency. Explore options that provide open APIs or built-in integrations with popular applications to maximize the utility of your AI investment.

Finally, take the time to research and compare different AI programs by reading reviews, seeking recommendations, and, if possible, participating in product demos. Gathering feedback from other small business owners or content creators can provide invaluable insights into the effectiveness of various tools. Additionally, many AI providers offer trial periods or freemium models, allowing you to test the software before fully committing. This hands-on experience can help you gauge how well the program meets your specific needs and whether it aligns with your operational workflow. By thoroughly evaluating your options, you can confidently select an AI solution that enhances your business performance and fosters sustainable growth.

3

AI-Powered Marketing Tools for Small Businesses

ESSENTIAL AI MARKETING TOOLS

In the evolving landscape of digital marketing, small business owners and content creators are increasingly turning to artificial intelligence (AI) to streamline their operations and enhance their strategies. AI marketing tools can transform how businesses reach and engage with their audiences, offering functionalities that were once accessible only to larger corporations with substantial budgets. These tools are designed to simplify complex processes, allowing small businesses to compete effectively in their respective markets. By integrating AI into their marketing efforts, entrepreneurs can harness data-driven insights, automate repetitive tasks, and create more personalized customer experiences.

One of the most significant advantages of AI marketing tools is their ability to optimize content creation and curation. For small businesses, maintaining a consistent online presence is crucial, yet creating high-quality content can be time-consuming. AI-powered content creation tools can generate blog posts, social media updates, and marketing copy tailored to a brand's voice and audience preferences. Furthermore, AI can assist in content curation by analyzing trends and user engagement to recommend relevant topics and formats, ensuring that business owners are always in tune with their audience's interests.

Effective inventory management is vital for small businesses, particularly those engaged in e-commerce. AI-enhanced inventory management systems can analyze sales patterns, predict demand, and optimize stock levels, helping businesses reduce costs and avoid stockouts or overstock situations. These systems leverage machine learning algorithms to forecast trends based on historical data, allowing owners to make informed decisions about purchasing and inventory turnover. By utilizing these tools, small business owners can enhance operational efficiency and focus on growth strategies rather than day-to-day inventory concerns.

Financial planning and budgeting are other critical aspects where AI tools can make a significant impact. AI-driven financial planning software can help small businesses analyze their financial health, forecast cash flow, and create actionable budgets. These tools can identify spending patterns, highlight potential savings, and even suggest investment opportunities based on the business's financial goals. By automating these processes, small business owners can gain deeper insights into their financial performance, enabling them to make strategic decisions that support sustainable growth.

Personalized email marketing automation is another area where AI excels, allowing small businesses to communicate more effectively with their customers. AI tools can segment audiences based on behavior and preferences, enabling personalized campaigns that resonate with individual recipients. By analyzing engagement metrics, these tools can also optimize send times and subject lines for maximum impact. This level of customization not only improves open and click-through rates but also fosters stronger customer relationships, ultimately driving sales and loyalty. By embracing AI marketing tools, small business owners and content creators can harness the power of technology to elevate their marketing efforts and achieve their growth objectives.

INTEGRATING AI TOOLS INTO YOUR MARKETING STRATEGY

Integrating AI tools into your marketing strategy can significantly enhance the efficiency and effectiveness of your efforts, particularly for small business owners and content creators. The first step in this integration process is understanding the various AI programs available that cater specifically to your needs. From AI-powered marketing tools that automate repetitive tasks to smart inventory management systems that optimize stock levels, identifying the right tools is crucial. Start by assessing your business goals and pinpointing areas where AI can alleviate pain points, such as content creation, customer engagement, and data analysis.

Once you have a clear understanding of the AI tools at your disposal, it is essential to align them with your marketing strategy. For instance, employing AI-based content creation and curation tools can streamline your content production processes. These tools can generate ideas, optimize content for SEO, and even assist in writing compelling copy. By leveraging AI-driven SEO optimization tools, you can enhance your online visibility and attract more relevant traffic to your website. This alignment ensures that every tool you implement serves a purpose and contributes to your overall marketing objectives.

Personalized email marketing automation is another area where AI can make a significant impact. With AI tools, you can analyze customer behavior and preferences to tailor your email campaigns effectively. This personalization not only boosts engagement rates but also fosters customer loyalty. By segmenting your audience and using predictive analytics, you can deliver the right message at the right time, leading to higher conversion rates. Incorporating AI into your email marketing strategy helps you create a more dynamic and responsive approach to customer communication.

In addition to enhancing customer engagement and content creation, AI tools can also optimize your financial planning and budgeting processes. AI-enhanced financial tools provide insights into cash flow, sales forecasts, and expense management, enabling you to make informed decisions. Small business owners can benefit from these insights by identifying trends and adjusting their strategies accordingly. Furthermore, AI-driven predictive analytics can help you anticipate market shifts and consumer demands, allowing you to stay ahead of the competition and adjust your marketing strategies proactively.

Lastly, integrating AI tools for social media management can streamline your online presence, ensuring consistent engagement across platforms. Virtual assistants can automate tasks such as posting schedules, responding to inquiries, and analyzing engagement metrics. By utilizing these tools, small business owners and content creators can focus more on strategic initiatives while maintaining an active and responsive online presence. Embracing AI in your marketing strategy not only enhances productivity but also empowers you to leverage data-driven insights, ultimately leading to sustained growth and success in a competitive marketplace.

4

AI-Based Content Creation and Curation

THE ROLE OF AI IN CONTENT CREATION

The integration of artificial intelligence in content creation has transformed the landscape for small businesses and content creators. By automating repetitive tasks and providing data-driven insights, AI tools enhance the efficiency and effectiveness of content production. Small business owners can leverage AI to streamline their workflows, freeing up valuable time to focus on creative strategies and customer engagement. AI-powered writing assistants can generate high-quality content quickly, enabling businesses to maintain a consistent online presence and meet the demands of their audience.

In addition to improving productivity, AI plays a crucial role in personalizing content for target audiences. Through advanced analytics, AI tools can analyze customer behavior, preferences, and engagement patterns. This data allows businesses to tailor their messaging and content strategies to resonate with specific demographics. For instance, AI algorithms can suggest topics and formats that are likely to engage particular customer segments, ensuring that content is both relevant and impactful. This level of personalization enhances customer loyalty and drives higher conversion rates.

Moreover, AI-based content curation tools help small business owners stay ahead of trends by identifying popular topics and relevant content across various platforms. These tools aggregate data from multiple sources, enabling businesses to curate content that aligns with their audience's interests. By sharing curated content, small businesses can position themselves as thought leaders in their industry while also saving time and resources in content discovery. This strategy not only enhances brand visibility but also fosters community engagement.

AI-driven SEO optimization tools further empower small businesses in their content creation efforts. By analyzing search trends and keyword performance, these tools provide actionable insights that can improve a website's search engine ranking. Small business owners can use these insights to create content that not only resonates with their audience but also meets the technical requirements of search engines. This dual focus on quality content and SEO best practices is essential for driving organic traffic and increasing online visibility.

Finally, the role of AI in content creation extends to social media management. AI tools can automate posting schedules, analyze engagement metrics, and even generate social media content.

This allows small business owners to maintain an active presence on various platforms without the constant need for manual oversight. Additionally, AI can provide predictive analytics that help businesses forecast trends and adjust their content strategies accordingly. As a result, small businesses can navigate the complexities of digital marketing with greater confidence and efficiency, ultimately fostering growth and success in an increasingly competitive landscape.

BEST PRACTICES FOR AI CONTENT CURATION

Effective content curation is essential for small business owners and content creators seeking to leverage AI technologies. One of the best practices for AI content curation involves selecting the right tools tailored to specific needs. Small businesses should explore AI-powered platforms that allow for streamlined content discovery, organization, and distribution. These tools can analyze user behavior, preferences, and engagement metrics, helping users identify which types of content resonate most with their audience. By utilizing these insights, businesses can enhance their content strategies while saving time and resources.

Another best practice is to maintain a consistent brand voice across curated content. AI tools can assist in achieving this by analyzing existing content to identify tone, style, and messaging patterns. When curating content from various sources, it is crucial to ensure that the selected pieces align with the brand's identity and values. This consistency not only reinforces brand recognition but also builds trust with the audience. Small business owners should take the time to review and edit curated content to ensure coherence with their messaging strategy.

Incorporating user-generated content (UGC) into the curation strategy is another effective practice. AI can help identify authentic UGC that aligns with the business's goals and audience interests. By showcasing customer testimonials, reviews, and creative uses of products, businesses can foster community engagement and trust. Additionally, UGC often comes with a built-in promotional advantage, as customers who see their content shared are more likely to spread the word about the brand. This approach not only enhances content diversity but also strengthens the relationship between the brand and its audience.

Regularly analyzing the performance of curated content is vital for ongoing improvement. Small business owners should leverage AI analytics tools to track engagement metrics, such as shares, likes, and comments, to determine what works best for their audience. This data-driven approach allows businesses to refine their content curation strategies over time. By understanding which types of content drive engagement, businesses can make informed decisions about future curation efforts and adapt their strategies accordingly.

Finally, fostering collaboration within the team is essential for maximizing the potential of AI content curation. Small business owners and content creators should encourage open communication about content ideas and curation strategies. By utilizing collaborative tools powered by AI, team members can share insights, track trends, and contribute to the content library more effectively. This collaborative effort not only enhances creativity but also ensures that the content curation process is efficient and aligned with the overall business goals.

5

Smart Inventory Management Systems

BENEFITS OF AI IN INVENTORY MANAGEMENT

The integration of artificial intelligence in inventory management presents numerous advantages for small business owners and content creators. One of the primary benefits is the enhancement of efficiency. AI systems can automate routine tasks, such as tracking stock levels and reordering products, which significantly reduces the manual workload. This automation allows businesses to allocate human resources to more strategic activities, such as marketing and customer engagement, ultimately driving growth and innovation.

Another significant advantage is the improvement in accuracy and forecasting capabilities. AI-powered inventory management systems utilize predictive analytics to analyze historical data and market trends, enabling businesses to make informed decisions regarding stock levels and timing. This reduces the risk of overstocking or stockouts, which can lead to lost sales and increased holding costs. By ensuring optimal inventory levels, small businesses can maintain a steady cash flow and enhance customer satisfaction through consistent product availability.

Furthermore, AI can facilitate better decision-making by providing real-time insights into inventory performance. Small business owners can access dashboards that display key metrics, such as turnover rates and seasonal demand fluctuations. This data-driven approach empowers owners to identify patterns and adjust their strategies accordingly. For instance, if an AI system indicates a decline in sales for a particular product, the business can quickly pivot its marketing efforts or promote alternative items to mitigate potential losses.

Cost reduction is another vital benefit of implementing AI in inventory management. By optimizing stock levels and reducing waste through accurate forecasting, businesses can lower holding costs and minimize markdowns on unsold inventory. Additionally, AI can analyze supplier performance and negotiate better terms based on data insights, further enhancing overall profitability. For small businesses that often operate on tighter margins, these savings can be crucial for long-term sustainability.

Lastly, AI enhances customer experiences through personalized services and improved order fulfillment. With advanced algorithms, businesses can analyze customer purchasing behavior and preferences, allowing for targeted marketing campaigns and tailored product recommendations. This personalization not only increases customer satisfaction but also fosters loyalty and repeat business. By streamlining inventory management with AI, small business owners can deliver exceptional service, ensuring their offerings align with customer needs and market demands.

IMPLEMENTING SMART INVENTORY SOLUTIONS

Implementing smart inventory solutions is essential for small business owners and content creators who seek to optimize their operations and enhance customer satisfaction. Traditional inventory management methods often fall short in providing the real-time insights necessary for making informed decisions. By leveraging AI-powered inventory management systems, businesses can automate their tracking processes, minimize human error, and gain visibility into stock levels, demand forecasts, and replenishment needs. This technology not only enhances operational efficiency but also allows for better alignment with marketing strategies and customer expectations.

AI-driven inventory management solutions utilize data analytics to predict trends and optimize stock levels. These systems analyze historical sales data, seasonal fluctuations, and market trends to forecast future demand accurately. By understanding these patterns, small business owners can avoid overstocking or understocking, which directly affects cash flow and customer satisfaction. This proactive approach enables businesses to maintain a balance between meeting customer demand and minimizing excess inventory costs, ultimately leading to improved profitability.

Incorporating smart inventory solutions also facilitates better supplier management. AI technologies can streamline the procurement process by identifying the best suppliers based on performance metrics such as delivery times, pricing, and quality. This ensures that small businesses can source materials and products efficiently, reducing lead times and enhancing overall operational agility. Moreover, automated inventory systems can send alerts when reordering is necessary, allowing owners to maintain optimum stock levels without the constant manual oversight that often leads to stress and errors.

For content creators, smart inventory solutions can be particularly beneficial in managing digital assets and merchandise. By implementing AI tools that track engagement and sales data, creators can gain insights into which products or content pieces resonate most with their audience. This data-driven approach allows for more targeted marketing efforts, ensuring that creators can focus on producing content that aligns with their audience's preferences. Additionally, inventory management systems can help in organizing promotional materials and merchandise, streamlining the selling process and enhancing the overall customer experience.

Integrating smart inventory solutions is a strategic move that empowers small businesses and content creators to harness the power of AI for growth and efficiency. By adopting these technologies, they can transform inventory management from a reactive process into a proactive strategy that not only meets customer needs but also supports long-term business objectives. As the landscape of small business operations continues to evolve, leveraging AI-driven inventory solutions will be crucial for maintaining a competitive edge and driving sustainable growth.

6

AI-Enhanced Financial Planning and Budgeting

TOOLS FOR AI FINANCIAL PLANNING

In the rapidly evolving landscape of small business management, AI financial planning tools have emerged as essential resources for entrepreneurs seeking to optimize their financial strategies. These tools leverage sophisticated algorithms and data analytics to provide insights that can significantly enhance budgeting, forecasting, and overall financial management. For small business owners and content creators, adopting AI-powered financial planning solutions can streamline operations and enable more informed decision-making, ultimately contributing to sustained growth and profitability.

One of the key advantages of AI financial planning tools is their ability to analyze vast amounts of data in real time. This capability allows small business owners to track their financial health more effectively by providing detailed reports on cash flow, expenses, and revenue trends. With features such as automated expense tracking and real-time financial dashboards, these tools enable users to identify patterns and anomalies that may impact their bottom line. By gaining a clearer understanding of their financial position, entrepreneurs can make proactive adjustments to their budgets and strategies, ensuring they remain agile in a competitive marketplace.

Predictive analytics is another powerful feature often integrated into AI financial planning tools. By utilizing historical data and market trends, these tools can forecast future financial scenarios, helping business owners anticipate challenges and seize opportunities. For instance, a small business might use predictive analytics to determine the optimal time to launch a new product based on seasonal spending patterns or customer behavior. This foresight not only aids in strategic planning but also allows for more effective resource allocation, ensuring that marketing efforts and inventory management align with projected financial outcomes.

Additionally, AI financial planning tools often include personalized budgeting features that cater to the unique needs of small businesses and content creators. These tools can suggest budget adjustments based on specific goals, such as increasing marketing spend during peak seasons or reallocating funds to address unexpected expenses. By tailoring budgeting strategies to individual business objectives, owners can optimize their financial resources and enhance their ability to invest in growth initiatives, such as AI-powered marketing tools and content creation solutions.

Finally, the integration of AI financial planning tools with other business management technologies offers a comprehensive approach to operational efficiency. Many platforms allow for seamless connections with inventory management systems, email marketing automation, and social media management tools. This interconnectedness not only enhances data accuracy but also facilitates a holistic view of business performance. By employing AI-driven financial planning alongside these other technologies, small business owners can cultivate a data-driven culture that drives innovation and improves overall business outcomes.

USING AI FOR BUDGET OPTIMIZATION

Using AI for budget optimization can significantly transform how small business owners manage their financial resources. By leveraging advanced algorithms and predictive analytics, AI tools can analyze historical spending patterns, forecast future financial trends, and identify areas where expenses can be reduced without sacrificing quality or productivity. This approach allows small business owners to make informed decisions based on data-driven insights, leading to more effective allocation of their budgets.

One of the primary advantages of AI in budget optimization is its ability to automate financial tracking and reporting. Traditional budgeting processes often involve manual data entry and analysis, which can be time-consuming and prone to errors. AI-powered financial tools streamline this process by automatically collecting and analyzing data from various sources, such as sales reports, marketing expenditures, and operational costs. This not only saves time but also enhances the accuracy of financial assessments, enabling business owners to quickly pinpoint discrepancies and adjust budgets accordingly.

Additionally, AI systems can provide insights into spending patterns and trends that may not be immediately apparent through manual analysis. By utilizing machine learning, these tools can identify recurring expenses that may be unnecessary or excessive. For example, a small business might discover that certain marketing campaigns yield a low return on investment, allowing owners to reallocate funds towards more effective strategies. This level of insight empowers business owners to optimize their budgets proactively rather than reactively, fostering a culture of continuous improvement.

Furthermore, AI can enhance financial forecasting by analyzing market trends, consumer behavior, and economic conditions. These predictive analytics capabilities enable small business owners to anticipate fluctuations in revenue and adjust their budgets accordingly. For instance, during peak seasons or economic downturns, AI tools can suggest optimal budget adjustments to ensure that cash flow remains stable. This proactive approach minimizes the risk of financial strain and allows businesses to capitalize on opportunities as they arise.

Finally, incorporating AI into budget optimization not only improves financial management but also frees up valuable time for small business owners to focus on strategic growth initiatives. By automating routine budgeting tasks and providing actionable insights, business owners can allocate more time to creative endeavors, marketing strategies, and customer engagement. As they harness the power of AI, small business owners can achieve a more sustainable financial footing, paving the way for long-term growth and success in an increasingly competitive landscape.

7

Personalized Email Marketing Automation

IMPORTANCE OF PERSONALIZATION IN EMAIL MARKETING

Personalization in email marketing has emerged as a critical strategy for small business owners and content creators looking to enhance customer engagement and drive conversions. In the crowded digital marketplace, where consumers receive countless promotional emails daily, personalized communication stands out as a key differentiator. By tailoring messages to individual preferences, behaviors, and demographics, businesses can foster stronger connections with their audience. This level of engagement not only increases open and click-through rates but also builds brand loyalty, encouraging repeat business and referrals.

The effectiveness of personalized email marketing lies in its ability to provide relevant content that resonates with the recipient. Small businesses can utilize AI-powered marketing tools to analyze customer data and segment their audience based on various criteria, such as purchasing history, interests, and interactions with previous emails. By leveraging this information, businesses can craft targeted campaigns that speak directly to the needs and desires of each segment. This not only enhances the customer experience but also maximizes the return on investment for marketing efforts, making every email sent more impactful.

Moreover, personalization goes beyond merely addressing the recipient by name. Advanced techniques such as dynamic content, tailored product recommendations, and behavior-triggered emails can significantly enhance the effectiveness of campaigns. For instance, an e-commerce business can send personalized recommendations based on a customer's past purchases or browsing behavior, increasing the likelihood of a sale. Similarly, for content creators, sending curated content that aligns with the interests of specific audience segments can deepen engagement and encourage further interaction.

As AI-driven tools continue to evolve, small business owners have access to sophisticated systems that streamline the personalization process. Automated email marketing platforms can analyze customer data in real-time, allowing businesses to adapt their messaging strategies quickly. This agility is particularly valuable in today's fast-paced environment, where consumer preferences can shift rapidly. By harnessing AI for personalized email marketing, small businesses can not only save time but also ensure that their communications remain relevant and timely.

In conclusion, the importance of personalization in email marketing cannot be overstated, particularly for small businesses and content creators striving for growth. By implementing personalized strategies, businesses can enhance customer engagement, improve conversion rates, and cultivate lasting relationships with their audience. As technology continues to advance, embracing these personalized approaches will not only set businesses apart from the competition but also pave the way for sustained success in an increasingly digital landscape.

TOOLS FOR AI-DRIVEN EMAIL CAMPAIGNS

In the age of digital marketing, email campaigns remain a cornerstone for small businesses and content creators aiming to build relationships with their audience. With the integration of artificial intelligence, these campaigns can be transformed into highly personalized and effective tools for driving engagement and conversions. AI-driven email marketing tools empower small business owners to automate processes, segment their audience more precisely, and analyze campaign performance in real time. This not only saves time but also enhances the quality of interactions with customers, leading to improved retention and sales.

One of the most vital tools for AI-driven email campaigns is automated segmentation software. This technology analyzes customer behavior, preferences, and demographics, allowing businesses to categorize their audience into distinct groups. By understanding the unique characteristics of each segment, small businesses can craft tailored messages that resonate more deeply with recipients. For instance, a small e-commerce store could segment its audience based on past purchase behavior, sending targeted promotions to customers who have shown interest in specific product categories. This level of personalization increases the chances of email opens and conversions significantly.

Another essential component of AI-driven email marketing is predictive analytics. These tools leverage historical data to forecast future customer behaviors, preferences, and trends. By implementing predictive analytics, small business owners can identify the best times to send emails, the types of content most likely to engage different segments, and even predict customer churn. This proactive approach allows businesses to not only react to customer needs but also anticipate them, creating a more satisfying customer experience. When businesses can predict what their audience wants, they can deliver it more effectively, thereby enhancing customer loyalty.

Furthermore, AI-powered content creation tools play a crucial role in email campaigns. By utilizing natural language processing and machine learning algorithms, these tools can generate engaging subject lines, email copy, and even personalized content based on recipient data. This not only streamlines the content creation process but also ensures that the messaging remains relevant and appealing. For instance, a content creator may use AI to automatically generate blog summaries or promotional emails that align with their latest content, saving time while maintaining high-quality communication with their audience.

Lastly, the integration of AI-driven analytics tools allows small business owners to monitor the performance of their email campaigns in real time. These tools provide insights into open rates, click-through rates, and conversion metrics, enabling business owners to assess what strategies work and what needs adjustment. By continuously analyzing this data, businesses can refine their email marketing tactics, experiment with different approaches, and ultimately drive better results. With AI at their disposal, small businesses can turn their email campaigns into powerful engines of growth, leveraging insights that were previously difficult to obtain.

8

AI Tools for Social Media Management

LEVERAGING AI FOR SOCIAL MEDIA SUCCESS

Leveraging AI for social media success represents a transformative opportunity for small business owners and content creators. In an era where social media platforms dominate the digital landscape, integrating artificial intelligence can streamline operations, enhance engagement, and drive measurable results. By harnessing AI-powered tools, businesses can automate repetitive tasks, analyze audience behavior, and optimize content strategies, ultimately leading to increased visibility and growth.

One of the primary benefits of AI in social media management is its ability to analyze vast amounts of data quickly. AI algorithms can sift through user interactions, engagement metrics, and demographic information to identify trends and preferences. This data-driven insight allows businesses to tailor their content to resonate with their target audience, ensuring that posts are not only relevant but also strategically timed for maximum impact. By leveraging predictive analytics, small business owners can anticipate shifts in consumer behavior, enabling them to adjust their social media strategies proactively.

Content creation is another area where AI can significantly enhance social media presence. AI-based tools can generate high-quality copy, suggest relevant hashtags, and even curate visual content that aligns with brand aesthetics. For small business owners who may lack the resources for dedicated content teams, these AI-driven solutions provide an efficient way to maintain a steady flow of engaging posts. Furthermore, AI can assist in A/B testing different types of content, allowing businesses to refine their messaging based on real-time performance data.

Engagement automation is essential for maintaining an active social media presence. AI tools can automate responses to common inquiries, schedule posts at optimal times, and monitor conversations around a brand. This not only saves time but also ensures that businesses remain responsive to their audience. By implementing AI-enhanced chatbots, small business owners can provide instant support, fostering a sense of connection with customers and enhancing overall brand loyalty.

Finally, leveraging AI for social media success involves continuously measuring and refining tactics based on performance analytics. AI-driven SEO optimization tools can help businesses improve their discoverability on social media platforms, while personalized email marketing automation can create tailored campaigns that drive traffic back to social channels. By integrating these AI strategies, small business owners and content creators can create a cohesive digital marketing ecosystem that not only boosts social media engagement but also contributes to long-term growth and sustainability.

SELECTING THE RIGHT SOCIAL MEDIA TOOLS

Selecting the right social media tools is crucial for small business owners and content creators looking to leverage AI technology for enhanced marketing strategies. With a plethora of options available, it can be overwhelming to determine which tools will best serve your specific needs. Begin by assessing your business objectives and target audience. Consider which platforms your audience frequents and the type of content that resonates with them. Identifying these factors will help narrow down your choices and ensure that the tools you select align with your marketing goals.

Once you have a clear understanding of your objectives, evaluate the features of various social media management tools. Look for functionalities that streamline content creation, scheduling, and performance analytics. Tools that offer AI-driven insights can help you optimize your posting schedule and content strategy based on audience engagement metrics. Additionally, features such as automated replies and chatbots can enhance customer interaction, allowing you to maintain a consistent presence across platforms without exhausting your resources.

Another important aspect to consider is the integration capabilities of the social media tools you are reviewing. Seamless integration with other AI-powered marketing tools you may already be using, such as email marketing automation and predictive analytics, can create a cohesive marketing ecosystem. This interconnectedness allows for better data sharing and a more unified approach to your marketing efforts, ultimately leading to more informed decision-making and improved business outcomes.

Cost is also a significant factor when selecting social media tools, especially for small businesses operating with limited budgets. Many tools offer tiered pricing models or free versions with essential features. It is advisable to start with tools that provide a trial period, enabling you to test their effectiveness without a long-term commitment. As your business grows, you can then explore more advanced features or premium versions that may better suit your evolving needs.

Finally, consider the level of support and resources provided by the tool's developers. Robust customer support, comprehensive tutorials, and an active community can significantly enhance your experience and help you maximize the tool's potential. Small business owners and content creators should prioritize tools that not only meet their immediate needs but also offer ongoing support and updates to adapt to the ever-changing landscape of social media marketing. By carefully choosing the right social media tools, you can effectively harness AI's power to drive engagement and growth for your business.

9

Predictive Analytics for Small Business Growth

UNDERSTANDING PREDICTIVE ANALYTICS

Predictive analytics is a crucial component of modern marketing strategies, particularly for small business owners and content creators looking to leverage artificial intelligence for growth.

At its core, predictive analytics involves using historical data, statistical algorithms, and machine learning techniques to identify the likelihood of future outcomes based on past events. For small businesses, this means transforming raw data into actionable insights that can inform decision-making, optimize marketing efforts, and enhance customer engagement.

Understanding the benefits of predictive analytics begins with recognizing its potential to drive smarter marketing campaigns. Small businesses often operate with limited resources and must prioritize their efforts to maximize ROI. By analyzing customer behavior and preferences, predictive analytics enables business owners to tailor their marketing strategies, ensuring that messages resonate with the right audience at the right time. This targeted approach not only improves customer acquisition rates but also fosters stronger relationships, ultimately leading to increased customer loyalty.

In addition to enhancing marketing campaigns, predictive analytics can significantly streamline inventory management. Small businesses often face challenges related to overstocking or stockouts, which can impact cash flow and customer satisfaction. By employing predictive models, business owners can forecast demand more accurately, allowing for better inventory planning and management. This not only reduces costs associated with excess inventory but also ensures that products are available when customers need them, enhancing the overall shopping experience.

Moreover, predictive analytics plays a vital role in financial planning and budgeting. Small business owners can leverage these analytics to analyze past financial performances and predict future trends, enabling more accurate forecasting and budgeting. By understanding seasonal variations and market fluctuations, businesses can allocate resources more effectively, minimizing risks and maximizing opportunities for growth. This proactive approach to financial management is essential for sustaining long-term success in an increasingly competitive landscape.

Lastly, predictive analytics can enhance personalized marketing efforts, particularly in email campaigns. By analyzing customer data, businesses can segment their audience and tailor content to meet specific needs and preferences. This level of personalization increases engagement rates and conversion rates, as customers are more likely to respond to messages that resonate with them. Additionally, predictive analytics can help identify the optimal times to send communications, further improving the effectiveness of email marketing strategies. For small business owners and content creators, embracing predictive analytics is not just a trend; it is a powerful tool for driving growth and achieving sustainable success.

APPLYING PREDICTIVE ANALYTICS TO BUSINESS STRATEGIES

Applying predictive analytics to business strategies offers small business owners and content creators a powerful tool to enhance decision-making and drive growth. Predictive analytics involves using historical data, statistical algorithms, and machine learning techniques to identify the likelihood of future outcomes based on past behavior. For small businesses, this means being able to anticipate customer needs, optimize marketing efforts, and streamline operations more efficiently than ever before.

One of the most significant applications of predictive analytics is in understanding customer behavior. By analyzing purchase history, online interactions, and demographic data, small business owners can create detailed customer profiles that reveal buying patterns and preferences. This information allows for the development of targeted marketing strategies, ensuring that promotions and communications resonate more deeply with specific audience segments. For content creators, this means tailoring content to match audience interests, which can significantly enhance engagement and conversion rates.

In addition to customer insights, predictive analytics can inform inventory management practices. By forecasting demand based on historical sales data, small businesses can optimize their stock levels, reducing waste and improving cash flow. Smart inventory management systems can automatically adjust orders based on predictive insights, ensuring that businesses can meet customer demands without overstocking. This operational efficiency not only saves money but also enhances customer satisfaction by minimizing stockouts and delays.

Financial planning and budgeting are other areas where predictive analytics can play a critical role. By analyzing trends and historical financial data, small business owners can create more accurate forecasts for revenue and expenses. This enables them to allocate resources more effectively and identify potential financial challenges before they arise. With AI-enhanced financial tools, businesses can continuously refine their budgets based on real-time data, making it easier to adapt to changing market conditions.

Lastly, predictive analytics can significantly enhance personalized marketing efforts, particularly in email marketing automation. By segmenting audiences based on predictive insights, small businesses can design personalized campaigns that are likely to resonate with each recipient. This targeted approach not only boosts engagement rates but also increases the likelihood of conversions. As small business owners integrate predictive analytics into their marketing strategies, they can expect improved ROI and stronger customer relationships, ultimately driving growth in today's competitive landscape.

10

AI-Driven SEO Optimization Tools

THE INTERSECTION OF AI AND SEO

The intersection of AI and SEO represents a transformative opportunity for small business owners and content creators looking to enhance their online visibility and engage effectively with their target audience. As search engines evolve, so too must the strategies employed to optimize content for these platforms. AI technologies, particularly in areas such as natural language processing and machine learning, are redefining how

SEO is approached. By leveraging these advancements, small businesses can not only improve their search rankings but also gain deeper insights into consumer behavior and preferences.

AI-powered SEO tools are revolutionizing keyword research and content optimization. Traditional methods often relied on manual analysis and guesswork, but AI algorithms can analyze vast amounts of data in real-time to identify trends and opportunities. These tools can suggest relevant keywords, analyze competitor strategies, and even predict shifts in search patterns. For small business owners, this means a more strategic approach to content creation, ensuring that their messaging aligns with what potential customers are actively searching for. The result is a more targeted and effective digital marketing strategy that can lead to increased traffic and conversions.

Content creation and curation are also greatly enhanced by AI technologies. AI-driven tools can assist in generating high-quality content that resonates with audiences, optimizing it for search engines simultaneously. For content creators, this means they can streamline their processes, reduce the time spent on mundane tasks, and focus on crafting compelling narratives that engage their audience. Furthermore, AI can curate content from various sources, allowing small businesses to remain relevant and informed about industry trends and consumer interests, thus positioning themselves as thought leaders in their niche.

In addition to content creation, AI plays a critical role in personalizing the user experience. By analyzing user behavior and preferences, AI can help small businesses tailor their websites and marketing strategies to meet the specific needs of their audience. This level of personalization not only improves user engagement but also enhances SEO performance, as search engines increasingly prioritize user experience as a ranking factor. Personalized email marketing automation powered by AI can deliver targeted messages to consumers, driving higher open and conversion rates, ultimately contributing to business growth.

Finally, predictive analytics fueled by AI can guide small businesses in making informed decisions that impact their SEO strategies. By forecasting trends and consumer behaviors, businesses can adapt their content and marketing efforts proactively rather than reactively. This forward-thinking approach allows small business owners to stay ahead of the competition and capitalize on emerging opportunities. As AI continues to evolve, its integration into SEO strategies will become increasingly critical for small businesses and content creators striving for sustainable growth in a digital landscape that is constantly changing.

TOP AI TOOLS FOR SEO ENHANCEMENT

In the ever-evolving landscape of digital marketing, search engine optimization (SEO) remains a cornerstone for small businesses and content creators looking to enhance their online visibility. The integration of artificial intelligence (AI) into SEO strategies has revolutionized the way businesses approach their online presence. AI-powered tools are no longer just optional; they have become essential for optimizing content, improving search rankings, and gaining insights into consumer behavior. Understanding and utilizing these tools can significantly elevate a small business's marketing efforts and drive organic traffic to their websites.

One of the most effective AI tools for SEO enhancement is keyword research software, which helps identify high-value keywords that potential customers are searching for. Tools like SEMrush, Ahrefs, and Moz use algorithms to analyze search trends, competition, and search volume, allowing users to make informed decisions about which keywords to target. By leveraging AI-driven insights, small business owners can create content that aligns with what their audience is actively seeking, ultimately leading to higher engagement and improved rankings on search engines.

Another powerful category of AI tools focuses on content optimization. Platforms like Clearscope and MarketMuse utilize AI to analyze top-ranking content for specific keywords and provide recommendations for enhancing the quality and relevance of your own content. These tools can suggest related topics, optimal word counts, and even readability scores. By using these insights, small businesses and content creators can produce high-quality, SEO-friendly content that resonates with their target audience, increasing the chances of ranking higher in search results.

Link-building remains a crucial aspect of SEO, and AI tools can streamline this process significantly. Tools such as LinkAssistant and BuzzSumo employ AI to identify potential backlink opportunities by analyzing competitor link profiles and tracking relevant industry mentions. This allows small business owners to focus their outreach efforts where they are most likely to yield results, thus enhancing their domain authority and search rankings. The automation of these tasks not only saves time but also maximizes the effectiveness of link-building strategies.

Lastly, AI analytics platforms are invaluable for monitoring and adjusting SEO strategies over time. Tools like Google Analytics and HubSpot use AI to provide in-depth insights into user behavior, traffic sources, and conversion rates. By analyzing this data, small business owners can identify which SEO strategies are working and which need refinement. Furthermore, predictive analytics can forecast trends and consumer behaviors, enabling businesses to stay ahead of the curve and adapt their content strategies accordingly. Embracing these AI tools for SEO enhancement not only optimizes online presence but also fosters sustained growth in an increasingly competitive digital marketplace.

11

Virtual Assistants for Task Automation and Product

BENEFITS OF USING VIRTUAL ASSISTANTS

The use of virtual assistants is transforming the way small businesses and content creators operate, offering a plethora of benefits that can streamline processes and enhance productivity.

Virtual assistants, powered by artificial intelligence, can manage routine tasks such as scheduling, data entry, and customer service inquiries. By automating these time-consuming activities, business owners can focus on strategic initiatives that drive growth and innovation. This shift not only improves operational efficiency but also allows for a more agile response to market changes.

One significant advantage of utilizing virtual assistants is the cost-effectiveness they offer. Hiring a full-time employee entails various expenses, including salaries, benefits, and training costs. In contrast, virtual assistants typically operate on a flexible basis, allowing businesses to pay only for the services they need. This model is particularly beneficial for small businesses and content creators who may have fluctuating workloads and require additional support during peak times without the long-term financial commitment associated with traditional hiring.

Furthermore, virtual assistants enhance scalability for small businesses. As a business grows, the demands on its resources increase, necessitating the need for additional support. Virtual assistants can be integrated into existing workflows with relative ease, providing the necessary assistance to manage increasing workloads. This scalability ensures that businesses can adapt quickly to changes in demand, whether it involves ramping up content production or managing customer interactions during busy seasons.

In addition to operational benefits, virtual assistants contribute to improved customer experience. By leveraging AI-powered tools, virtual assistants can provide prompt and accurate responses to customer inquiries, enhancing satisfaction and loyalty. This capability is particularly important for content creators who rely on audience engagement. With virtual assistants handling routine customer interactions, creators can devote more time to developing high-quality content and building deeper connections with their audience.

Lastly, the integration of virtual assistants into marketing strategies can lead to more effective campaigns. By utilizing AI-driven analytics, virtual assistants can gather insights on consumer behavior and preferences, enabling businesses to tailor their marketing initiatives accordingly. This data-driven approach not only enhances the effectiveness of marketing efforts but also allows for more personalized communication with customers. As small business owners and content creators navigate the complexities of marketing in a digital landscape, the strategic use of virtual assistants can provide a competitive edge, driving both growth and profitability.

CHOOSING THE RIGHT VIRTUAL ASSISTANT TOOLS

Choosing the right virtual assistant tools is essential for small business owners and content creators looking to streamline their operations and enhance productivity. The first step in this process is to identify the specific tasks and functions that a virtual assistant can handle. Whether it involves customer service inquiries, social media management, or content scheduling, understanding the unique needs of your business will help narrow down the options available. A clear assessment of your requirements will not only guide you in selecting the most appropriate tools but also ensure that your investment yields the best possible return.

Once you have a clear understanding of your needs, the next phase is to evaluate the features of various virtual assistant tools. Many platforms offer a wide range of functionalities, including task automation, integration with existing systems, and user-friendly interfaces. For instance, tools that specialize in AI-driven SEO optimization can enhance your online presence and increase traffic to your site. Additionally, AI-powered marketing tools can assist in personalizing email campaigns and targeting specific audiences, making them invaluable for small business growth. Prioritizing tools that align with your strategic goals will be crucial in maximizing their effectiveness.

Another important consideration is the scalability of the virtual assistant tools you choose. As your business grows, your operational needs may evolve, requiring tools that can adapt to increased demands. Look for solutions that offer flexible pricing models, additional features for advanced users, and integration options with other platforms. This adaptability will not only save you the hassle of frequently changing tools but will also ensure that you can continue to meet your business objectives without interruption.

User support and community resources also play a vital role in the selection process. Opt for tools that provide comprehensive customer service, including tutorials, forums, and responsive support teams. A strong support system can significantly reduce the learning curve associated with new technologies, allowing you to implement them effectively and efficiently. Additionally, engaging with user communities can offer insights and best practices that enhance your overall experience and help you make the most of the tools at your disposal.

Finally, considering the long-term impact of the virtual assistant tools on your business operations is essential. Look for tools that not only address immediate needs but also contribute to your overall growth strategy. Predictive analytics tools can provide valuable insights into customer behavior and market trends, allowing you to make informed decisions. By investing in virtual assistant tools that support both current opera-tions and future growth, small business owners and content creators can ensure a sustainable path forward in an increasingly competitive landscape.

12

Future Trends in AI for Small Businesses

EMERGING AI TECHNOLOGIES

Emerging AI technologies are revolutionizing the landscape for small businesses and content creators, providing innovative tools that enhance productivity, streamline operations, and personalize customer engagement. As small business owners and content creators seek to remain competitive in an increasingly digital marketplace, understanding these advancements is crucial. From AI-powered marketing tools to smart inventory management systems, the integration of artificial intelligence into business strategies can lead to significant growth and efficiency.

One of the most impactful areas of AI technology is in marketing automation. AI-powered marketing tools can analyze customer data and behavior patterns to create personalized marketing campaigns that resonate with target audiences. For small business owners, this means the ability to tailor promotions and communications based on individual preferences, leading to higher engagement rates and improved customer satisfaction. By leveraging AI for personalized email marketing automation, businesses can craft messages that speak directly to the needs and interests of their customers, thereby increasing conversion rates.

In addition to marketing, AI is transforming content creation and curation. AI-based content generation tools can assist creators in producing high-quality written content, graphics, and videos at a much faster pace. These technologies can suggest topics based on trending data, generate outlines, and even draft entire articles, enabling content creators to focus more on strategy and creativity. Furthermore, AI-driven SEO optimization tools can analyze search engine algorithms and user behavior to enhance content visibility, ensuring that small businesses can reach their intended audience more effectively.

Smart inventory management systems powered by AI are also becoming essential for small businesses. These systems utilize predictive analytics to forecast inventory needs based on historical data and market trends, helping business owners manage stock levels efficiently. By minimizing overstock and stockouts, small businesses can reduce carrying costs and improve cash flow. Additionally, AI-enhanced financial planning tools provide owners with insights into budgeting and financial forecasting, enabling informed decisions that drive profitability.

Finally, the significant role of virtual assistants in task automation and productivity cannot be overstated. AI-driven virtual assistants are invaluable tools that can assist small business owners in efficiently managing their daily tasks, scheduling appointments, and responding to customer inquiries. This support frees up valuable time, enabling entrepreneurs to concentrate on strategic growth initiatives that drive their businesses forward. With their advanced capabilities to analyze vast amounts of data and provide actionable insights, these tools empower business owners and content creators alike to make more informed decisions, optimize their operations, and enhance overall efficiency. As AI technologies continue to develop and improve, embracing these innovative solutions will be crucial for sustaining growth and achieving long-term success in the increasingly competitive landscape of small business. The future of entrepreneurship will undoubtedly be shaped by the effective integration of these intelligent systems.

PREPARING FOR THE FUTURE OF AI IN MARKETING

As the landscape of marketing continues to evolve with the advent of artificial intelligence, small business owners and content creators must proactively prepare for the future. Understanding the various AI programs available can significantly enhance operational efficiency, improve customer engagement, and ultimately drive growth. To successfully navigate this new terrain, it is essential to familiarize oneself with the range of AI-powered marketing tools specifically designed for small businesses. These tools can automate repetitive tasks, analyze data trends, and provide insights that were previously only accessible to larger enterprises with expansive resources.

An effective strategy begins with identifying the AI tools that best suit your business needs. Small business owners should assess their current marketing efforts and pinpoint areas where AI could streamline processes. For instance, AI-based content creation and curation tools can help generate relevant content faster while maintaining quality. By integrating these solutions, businesses can enhance their online presence without the burden of extensive labor. Additionally, adopting smart inventory management systems powered by AI can optimize stock levels, ensuring that businesses meet customer demand without incurring unnecessary costs.

Financial planning and budgeting are crucial for sustainable growth, and AI-enhanced systems offer significant advantages here. By leveraging predictive analytics, small businesses can make informed decisions based on data-driven forecasts. This capability allows owners to anticipate market shifts and adjust their strategies accordingly. Integrating AI tools for personalized email marketing automation can also create targeted campaigns that resonate with audiences, leading to higher conversion rates. Understanding customer behaviors and preferences through AI insights is essential for crafting messages that engage and convert.

Social media management is another area where AI can play a transformative role. With various AI tools available, small business owners can streamline their social media strategies, automate posting schedules, and analyze engagement metrics effectively. These insights help in refining marketing approaches and ensuring that content reaches the right audience at the right time.

Moreover, AI-driven SEO optimization tools can enhance online visibility, making it easier for potential customers to discover products and services. By investing in these technologies, businesses can stay competitive and relevant in a fast-paced digital environment.

Lastly, embracing virtual assistants for task automation and productivity can free up valuable time for small business owners and content creators. These AI-driven assistants can handle routine tasks, allowing entrepreneurs to focus on strategic initiatives and creative pursuits. As the marketing landscape shifts towards increased reliance on AI, it is imperative for small businesses to not only adopt these technologies but also to continuously educate themselves on emerging trends. By preparing for the future of AI in marketing, small business owners can position themselves for success in a rapidly changing marketplace.